WORKING WITH GRAMMAR

HOW TO BREAK IT DOWN & MAKE IT WORK FOR YOU!

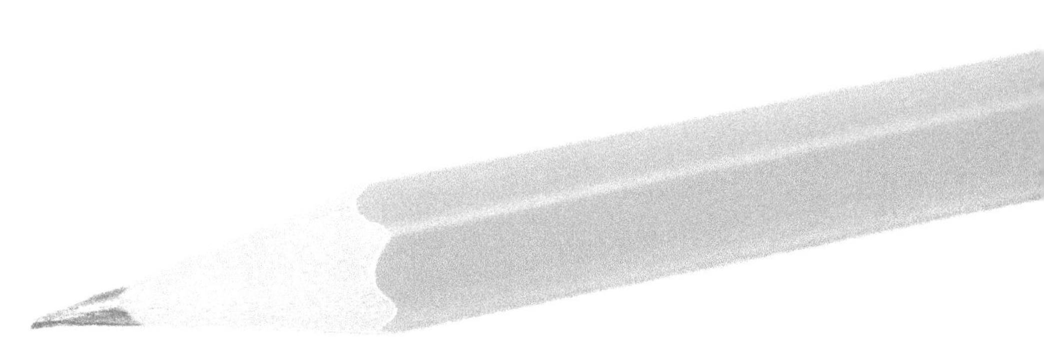

WORKING WITH GRAMMAR

HOW TO BREAK IT DOWN & MAKE IT WORK FOR YOU!

Published by
Heron Books, Inc.
20950 SW Rock Creek Road
Sheridan, OR 97378

heronbooks.com

Special thanks to all the teachers and students who provided feedback instrumental to this edition.

ISBN: 978-0-89739-117-7

Printed in the USA

10 June 2021

At Heron Books, we think learning should be engaging and fun. It should be hands-on and allow students to move at their own pace.

To facilitate this, we have created learning guides that will help any student progress through this book, chapter by chapter, with confidence and interest.

Get learning guides at
heronbooks.com/learningguides.

For a final exam, email
teacherresources@heronbooks.com

We would love to hear from you!
Email us at *feedback@heronbooks.com.*

Contents

PART 1
NOUNS AND PRONOUNS

PART 2
VERBS

PART 3
OTHER PARTS OF SPEECH

PART 4
THE SENTENCE

PART 5
JOBS NOUNS AND PRONOUNS DO IN SENTENCES

PART 6

WHAT IS CASE?

Introduction

Though more people speak Chinese and Spanish, English is possibly the most important language in the world today. With a huge vocabulary that allows a person to express almost any idea, it is now being used by people in almost every corner of the world.

Whether it is the language you grew up with or a second or third language that you are still trying to master, it can be both challenging and fun to understand how its different parts work together, which is the subject of English grammar.

Unfortunately, many students have become convinced that they don't like grammar and that it is a difficult subject to understand—usually the result of poor instruction or confusing textbooks.

Learning English grammar doesn't have to be hard.

Grammar is simply how words are put together so they make sense.

Working with Grammar, How to Break It Down & Make It Work for You!, along with its accompanying workbook, has been designed to help anyone master English grammar

one confident step at a time.

Ready for some challenge and fun?

—Editors

PART 1

NOUNS AND PRONOUNS

GRAMMAR?

Many people, young and old, have the idea that grammar is hard or that it's a subject they don't like. If you are one of those people, here's something to think about:

Maybe the reason it didn't go well has nothing to do with you.

Maybe the problem was with the book or class or teacher.

You don't have to like grammar as your favorite subject, but it isn't actually hard. Grammar is just how words are put together so that they make sense. That's all.

Again, **grammar** is simply

how words are put together so that they make sense.

Most of learning grammar just comes from listening to people who speak it correctly and reading books that are well written. If you read and listen to people who use English well, you will learn what sounds right.

You will also end up speaking and writing with good grammar.

So, you've already started your first grammar lesson:

Try to speak a lot with people who use English well, and read lots of well-written books. And by doing a lot of reading aloud, you will hear how words go together to make interesting and effective communication. (Plus, reading aloud can be a lot of fun!)

And that brings us to the second lesson about grammar:

The goal of learning anything about grammar is not to have perfect grammar. The goal is communication.

It's important to keep this in mind. When you are learning more information about how words are best put together in English, you're doing it so that you can speak, read and write better, or so you can better understand what someone else is trying to say or write.

Grammar is for helping communication and understanding. If it's not helping communication and understanding, it's a waste of time!

If you don't like grammar or got the idea that it's hard, somebody was probably making it harder than it is, or they just weren't teaching well. Grammar is simply how words are put together to make sense.

CONCLUSION

1. The best way to master grammar is by reading lots of well-written books and doing a lot of reading aloud.

2. The goal of learning about grammar is not to have perfect grammar. The goal is communication and understanding.

EXERCISE 1

SENTENCES & PARTS OF SPEECH

We usually say that a **sentence** is a group of words that expresses a *complete thought*.

> *Don't like*. (This is not a complete thought. It's not a sentence.)
>
> *I don't like the way you talk about Suzette.* (This makes sense. It's a complete thought and an actual sentence in English.)

The other simple description of a sentence is that *it has a subject and a verb*. There are usually other words that describe and explain more, but you have to have a subject and a verb for a normal English sentence.

Let's take a look:

He	plays	soccer.
(subject)	(verb)	(other word)

The sleepy student	yawned	loudly.
(subject)	(verb)	(other word)

You probably noticed that the main word of the subject is a noun. It's the noun the sentence is built on. It's the noun the sentence is about.

William	shot	the arrow	across the field.
(Noun, subject)	(verb)	(noun, but not subject)	(other words)

Arya	forgot	his bike.
(Noun, subject)	(verb)	(noun, but not the subject)

This book will talk a lot about subjects and verbs. They are the most basic parts of sentences.

WORDS

Every word in a sentence has some kind of job to do. Some words name things, others show action or being, still others describe things, and so on. Understanding how words go together requires understanding the different jobs they do.

The names of the jobs that words do are called *parts of speech.*

PARTS OF SPEECH

When you *speak*, there are *parts*.

Yes, sentences and words are parts of speaking (and writing). But **parts of speech** are what the words are *doing*, what *jobs* they have. We've already talked about two examples: nouns and verbs.

Words with the job of naming something are **nouns**. Nouns are a part of speech. *Dog* is a noun because it has the job of naming a type of animal.

All words that name people, places or things—even things you can't touch—are nouns, such as *James, New York, apple, house* and *happiness*.

Words with the job of showing action or being are **verbs**. Verbs are a part of speech. *Eat, run, think, grow, have* and *be* are verbs.

Sometimes the same word can have a different definition and job, depending on how it is used in a sentence. Let's look, for example, at the word *box*:

EXAMPLES	EXPLANATION
A *box* came in the mail.	In this sentence *box* is a thing, so it is a noun.
The boy can *box* like a professional.	Here, *box* is an action, so it is a verb.

Nouns and verbs are the two most basic parts of speech. Once they are understood well, there are six others one should understand, and all of them will be covered in this book.

EXERCISES
2–3

NOUNS

As you know, **nouns** are words that name a person, place, thing or idea. There are two main categories of nouns.

COMMON NOUNS

First there are **common nouns**, which name a general type of thing.

Here are some common nouns:

woman, man, holiday, state, country, freedom

They are only capitalized when they are the first word in a sentence.

Most nouns have two spellings depending on whether they are singular or plural. Usually an *s* is added to make a plural noun.

For example, *girl* becomes *girls*, and *table* becomes *tables.*

Some plural nouns change in different ways.

For example, *mouse* becomes *mice*, and *child* becomes *children.*

If the plural spelling of a noun is different from adding an *s*, most dictionaries will show it after the entry word.

PROPER NOUNS

The second category of noun is the **proper noun**, which names a particular person, place, or thing.

Here are examples of proper nouns:

> *Mary Jones, Robert Bailey, New Year, Oregon, France, Kleenex®, the Statue of Liberty*

Proper nouns are capitalized.

EXERCISES 4–10

PRONOUNS

Another part of speech is the **pronoun**. It is a word that *takes the place of a noun.*

We use pronouns so we don't need to repeat the names of things over and over. Compare the examples below where the pronouns *he, her* and *it* are used.

WITH NOUNS	WITHOUT NOUNS
Mrs. Jones threw the ball to the dog and the dog caught the ball.	Mrs. Jones threw the ball to the dog and *he* caught *it*.
Where is Mary's flower? The man gave the flower to Mary.	Where is Mary's flower? The man gave *it* to *her*.

When you're using pronouns, you will make your sentences clear if you use a singular pronoun when the noun it replaces is singular.

Similarly, a pronoun would be plural if the noun it replaces is plural.

UNCLEAR	CLEAR
My mother knows how to sew well, but *they* didn't make my prom dress.	My mother knows how to sew well, but *she* didn't make my prom dress.
When I finished reading the letter, I threw *them* away.	When I finished reading the letter, I threw *it* away.

UNCLEAR	CLEAR
Anya saw the shoes in the store and decided to try *it* on.	Anya saw the shoes in the store and decided to try *them* on.
Tom and John went to the game together and *he* enjoyed it.	Tom and John went to the game together and *they* enjoyed it.

There are six types of pronouns. We'll talk about them in the next sections.

PERSONAL PRONOUNS

Personal pronouns are used instead of the name of a person or a thing.

They are:

I	*me*	*you*	*he*	*him*	*she*
her	*it*	*we*	*us*	*they*	*them*

Here are some examples:

I went to see *him*.

What will *you* give *him* for his birthday?

Will *you* come with *us* to the concert?

We aren't going to go to the party, but *they* are.

Possessive pronouns are a type of personal pronoun that shows ownership.

They are:

mine *yours* *his* *hers*

its *ours* *theirs*

Here are some examples:

That computer is *mine.*

Please take *yours.*

Are those students' computers charged? *Theirs* are charged.

Those jerseys are *ours.*

EXERCISES 11–17

REFLEXIVE PRONOUNS

Reflexive means reflecting or turning back. **Reflexive pronouns** refer back to someone or something in the sentence. These pronouns end with *-self* or *-selves.* Sometimes reflexive pronouns are used just for emphasis.

Reflexive pronouns are:

myself *yourself* *himself* *herself* *oneself*

itself *ourselves* *yourselves* *themselves*

Here are some examples of reflexive pronouns in sentences:

I did it *myself.*

The bolt worked *itself* loose.

We fixed *ourselves* sandwiches for lunch.

The boys gave *themselves* a treat after the game.

I *myself* took those photographs. (emphasizes *I*)

We vow that we *ourselves* will be responsible for the children in our care. (emphasizes *we*)

EXERCISES 18–20

DEMONSTRATIVE PRONOUNS

Demonstrative means showing. **Demonstrative pronouns** show or point out someone or something.

There are four of them. Two are singular and two are plural:

Singular:	*this*	*that*
Plural:	*these*	*those*

Now for some examples in sentences:

This is my new phone.

Give me *that*.

Where did you buy *these*?

Those belong to Jane.

EXERCISES 21–23

INTERROGATIVE PRONOUNS

Interrogative means asking a question. **Interrogative pronouns** are used in place of a noun when asking a question.

There are five of them:

who *whom* *which* *whose* *what*

Here are some examples:

Who lives next door?

To *whom* did you give the book?

There are two kinds of tea. *Which* do you prefer?

Whose is that?

What is the name of your favorite movie?

EXERCISES 24–27

RELATIVE PRONOUNS

Relative means related or connected in meaning. **Relative pronouns** relate a descriptive group of words to a noun or pronoun mentioned earlier.

The most common relative pronouns are:

who *whom* *which* *what* *that*

Now for some examples:

The boy ***who** won the race* is fourteen years old.

The shirt, ***which** is on sale*, is green and white.

The gift was exactly ***what** he wanted.*

Jennifer got the puppy ***that** she liked* for her birthday.

(We use *who* for people and *that* for things.)

You'll probably notice that *who, whom, which*, and *what* are also listed as interrogative pronouns if they are used to ask a question. That's because the way a pronoun is used determines which type it is. Relative pronouns aren't used to ask a question.

Note: Some grammar references, not all, include *whose, whoever,* and *whomever* as relative pronouns.

EXERCISES
28–32

INDEFINITE PRONOUNS

Indefinite means not referring to a specific person or thing. **Indefinite pronouns** refer generally to people or things without naming the exact one. There are many of these.

Here are some common ones:

all	*everyone*	*other*
another	*everything*	*others*
any	*few*	*several*
anybody	*many*	*some*
anyone	*nobody*	*somebody*
anything	*no one*	*someone*
both	*none*	*something*
each	*nothing*	
everybody	*one*	

Here are a few examples:

All of the students are going to the game.

Few will take that test.

I will bring *something* that *everyone* will like.

Nothing tastes better than freshly baked, warm cookies.

When using an indefinite pronoun as the subject in a sentence, you need to know if the pronoun is singular or plural so the verb of the sentence is the same.

Here are some indefinite pronouns that are singular and need a singular verb:

anybody	*everything*	*someone*
anyone	*nobody*	*something*
each	*no one*	
everybody	*nothing*	
everyone	*somebody*	

Here are some common indefinite pronouns that are plural and use a plural verb:

both	*many*
few	*several*

Here are some common indefinite pronouns that can be either singular or plural:

all	*more*	*some*
any	*most*	*none*

To be clear, ensure the pronouns and verbs are both singular or both plural.

UNCLEAR	CLEAR
Plan for extra people at the party in case *several* (plural pronoun) brings (singular verb) their friends.	Plan for extra people at the party in case *several* (plural pronoun) bring (plural verb) their friends.
Everyone (singular pronoun) are (plural verb) bringing their own food to the picnic.	*Everyone* (singular pronoun) is (singular verb) bringing their own food to the picnic.

PRONOUN PLACEMENT

To make writing easier to understand, when using a pronoun, you'll want to place it so it clearly refers to the noun it is replacing. Sometimes, this means you might have to reword a sentence.

UNCLEAR	CLEARER
The teacher assigned the attendance job to Sarah Morgan because *she* felt it was the most important one in the class. (Did the teacher or Sarah Morgan feel the job was the most important one?)	The teacher felt the attendance job was the most important one in the class so *she* assigned it to Sarah Morgan.

This is especially true for relative pronouns. You'll want to pay extra attention to make sure the relative pronoun is placed nearest to the noun or pronoun it refers to, instead of being near some other noun in the sentence.

UNCLEAR	CLEARER
Allison, the granddaughter of Mrs. Taylor, *who* went to private school, was accepted at her favorite university. (Did the granddaughter or Mrs. Taylor go to private school?)	Mrs. Taylor's granddaughter, Allison, *who* went to private school, was accepted at her favorite university.

EXERCISES 33–40

PART 2

VERBS

VERBS

As you know, a **verb** is a word that tells what is happening or existing in a sentence. Every complete sentence has at least one verb.

There are two types of verbs. These are action and being verbs.

ACTION VERBS

Action verbs communicate about physical action, mental action, or possession. Take a look at the following examples.

ACTION VERBS	TYPE OF ACTION SHOWN
Austin *ran* to the store. Tony *jumps* higher than anyone else does. Joe *found* his sister in the gym. I *threw* the ball as hard as I could. Maggie *eats* salad every day.	physical action
I *remember* now where I left my keys. She *thinks* about her grandmother all the time. Jenny *considers* that her sister is her best friend. The student *decided* to do a community service project.	mental action

ACTION VERBS	TYPE OF ACTION SHOWN
My uncle *owns* two clothing stores.	
I *have* a racing bicycle.	possession
Noreen *kept* the doll she had.	
She *possesses* a beautiful voice.	

BEING VERBS

A **being verb** is a word that tells what or how something is.

The most common being verb is *be*. Another common one is *become*.

BEING VERBS	SENTENCES TELL WHAT OR HOW SOMETHING IS
Ann *is* a lawyer.	What is Ann? *a lawyer*
I *am* the art teacher.	What am I? *the art teacher*
They *are* programmers.	What are they? *programmers*
The game *was* very exciting.	How was the game? *exciting*
Please *be* quieter.	How should you be? *quieter*
They *were* intelligent.	How were they? *intelligent*
Will Joanne *become* a chef?	What could Joanne become? *a chef*
The woods *became* silent.	How did the woods become? *silent*

There are some being verbs that tell what things are like or how they appear. Some of these are:

seem *appear* *feel* *taste* *smell*

look *sound*

OTHER BEING VERBS	TELL WHAT THINGS ARE LIKE OR HOW THEY APPEAR
Andre *seems* happy today.	How did Andre *seem* today? *happy*
The canary *appears* to be ill.	How did the canary *appear*? *ill*
Kelsey *feels* that course is too easy.	How did Kelsey *feel* about the course? *It was too easy.*
This pizza *smells* delicious.	What did the pizza *smell* like? delicious
That cake *tastes* great.	What did the cake *taste* like? *great*
Ashley *sounds* excited.	How did Ashley *sound*? *excited*
It *looked* good to me.	How did it *look*? *good*

Seem is always a being verb but the other words in this group can also act as action verbs. Below you can see some examples of verbs that can act as an action verb or a being verb.

ACTING AS A BEING VERB	ACTING AS AN ACTION VERB
The canary *appears* to be ill.	Ellen *appears* in the lead role in that new play.
The cookies *smelled* wonderful as they were baking.	The baker *smelled* the cookies burning.
That board *feels* rough.	You can *feel* how smooth the table is.

ACTING AS A BEING VERB	ACTING AS AN ACTION VERB
That *sounds* exciting.	The bell *sounds* every day at noon.
Your painting *looks* beautiful.	He *looked* everywhere for his notebook.

EXERCISES 1–7

TWO OR MORE VERBS WORKING TOGETHER

Sometimes two or more verbs can be used together to express the action or being in a sentence.

EXAMPLE SENTENCES	SHOW ACTION OR BEING
Taka *is achieving* his goals.	The verb *is achieving* shows that Taka is doing something.
Amy *will sing* in the school play.	*Will sing* is the action that Amy will do.
Maddie *had been* there all day.	The verb *had been* shows that Maddie was being there.
As he treated more and more patients, John *was becoming* an excellent doctor.	*Was becoming* communicates what John was being.

There are several verbs that can work with another verb.* Take a look at them below.

THE VERBS THAT CAN WORK WITH ANOTHER VERB	EXAMPLES
be: *be, is, am, are, was, were, being, been*	She *was going* home. The boys *were thinking* about breakfast. The baby *is being fed.*

* Optional note: When one of these verbs works with another verb in a sentence, some grammar references call it a *helping verb* or an *auxiliary verb*.

THE VERBS THAT CAN WORK WITH ANOTHER VERB	EXAMPLES
do: *do, does, did*	John *does read* a lot. We *did see* that movie.
have: *have, has, had*	I *have washed* my hair. They *had* already *eaten.*
These can also work with another verb in a sentence:	
shall, will, would, should, can, could, may, might, must, ought	I *shall sing* in the show. This *might be* the biggest day of my life. Sean *could call* on his phone. The little girl *should* never *eat* peanuts. You *must open* that box.

Sometimes you will see these verbs separated by another word.

EXAMPLE SENTENCES	HOW THE VERBS WERE SEPARATED
Will Arnie *meet* Betty at the dance?	In sentences that ask a question, multiple verbs are usually separated by another word. In this example, the verb is *will meet*. *Arnie* is the subject of the question and not a part of the verb.
The Dragons *were* clearly *winning* the game.	The verb is *were winning*, which communicates the action of the sentence. *Clearly* describes how they were winning.
The neighbors *will* soon *be* home.	The verb is *will be*. It is separated by *soon*.
We *did* not *see* her there.	The word *not* isn't part of the verb *did see*. It makes the verb negative.

TWO OR MORE VERBS FOR THE SAME SUBJECT

Some sentences have two or more separate verbs saying different things about the same subject. Both action and being verbs can be used this way.

Here are some examples:

Garrett *swims*, *jogs* and *lifts* weights for exercise.

That rose *looks* and *smells* like the perfect rose.

The writer *researched* and *rewrote* that chapter three times.

J.R.R. Tolkien *decided* to write a book and later *became* a great author.

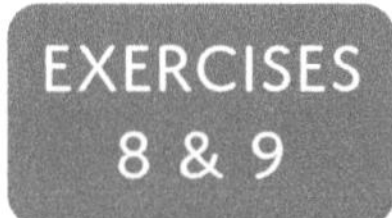

TRANSITIVE AND INTRANSITIVE VERBS

TRANSITIVE VERBS

A **transitive verb** expresses an action being received by someone or something.

The someone or something receiving the action is called a **direct object**.

Here are two transitive verbs in sentences.

Zelly likes his brother.
Zelly likes who? his *brother* (direct object)

Zaya wrote an email.
Zaya wrote what? an *email* (direct object)

A transitive verb is always an action verb that has a direct object. So, you can see if a verb is transitive by checking if it has a direct object receiving the action of the verb. Let's look at some examples.

SENTENCE WITH A TRANSITIVE VERB	DIRECT OBJECT
Leslie *drives* a car.	What does Leslie drive? She drives a car, so *car* is the direct object.
Suko *has* a cat.	What does Suko have? He has a cat, so *cat* is the direct object.

SENTENCE WITH A TRANSITIVE VERB	DIRECT OBJECT
Javier *plays* the violin.	What does Javier play? He plays the violin, so *violin* is the direct object.
The dog *smelled* the meat.	What did the dog smell? She smelled the meat, so *meat* is the direct object.

Notice that a direct object usually comes right after the transitive verb.

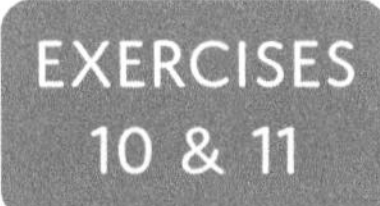

INTRANSITIVE VERBS

On the other hand, an **intransitive verb** never has a direct object. It simply communicates that the action or existence occurs.

Being verbs are always intransitive because they say how or what something is. They don't say that an action is happening to someone or something, a direct object.

Being verbs never have direct objects, so they are always intransitive. Take a look at these examples.

SENTENCE	INTRANSITIVE BEING VERBS
I *am* a fireman.	In this sentence, the noun *fireman* restates *I* and doesn't receive any action or ownership.

SENTENCE	INTRANSITIVE BEING VERBS
The truck *was* bright red.	*Bright red* describes the truck and is not a direct object.
Those cookies *smell* good.	This sentence is describing what the cookies are like. The cookies are not performing the action of smelling. Words such as *smell*, *look*, *taste* are being verbs when used in this way.

An action verb can be intransitive when the action, ownership or result it communicates doesn't happen to a direct object.

Look at how that works in these examples.

SENTENCE	INTRANSITIVE ACTION VERBS
My alarm clock *broke*.	*Broke* is intransitive because there is no direct object—nothing receives the action of the verb.
The Portuguese fisherman *rowed* for hours.	*Rowed* is intransitive. The sentence doesn't say that the fisherman *rowed* a boat or anything else, so there is no direct object.
Giselle *looked* around frantically.	*Looked* is intransitive because there is no direct object.

Actually many action verbs can be transitive or intransitive depending on the sentence. Let's compare the following pairs of sentences.

INTRANSITIVE	TRANSITIVE
Alice *sings* well.	Alice *sings* a song.
The musician *plays* beautifully.	The musician *plays* his instrument every day.
Annie *screamed* in delight.	Annie *screamed* thanks to Bob.

An intransitive verb can be followed by other words, but not a direct object.

SENTENCE WITH AN INTRANSITIVE VERB	EXPLANATION
He *ran* after the car.	*After the car* tells where he ran, so *ran* is an intransitive verb.
The children *played* enthusiastically.	*Played* is an intransitive verb here because *enthusiastically* describes how the children played.
The children *played* with the ball.	*Ball* may seem to be a direct object but *with the ball* describes how they *played*. That means *played* is an intransitive verb here because it has no direct object.

EXERCISES
12–18

SUBJECT-VERB AGREEMENT

As you know, the noun or pronoun a sentence is about is the subject. When writing a sentence, the verb should **agree** with the subject of the sentence. In grammar, *agree* means to have the correct spelling that fits in the sentence.

For example, you would say, *she laughs a lot,* not *she laugh a lot.*

In grammar, *person* means who the speaker is talking about:

In *first person*, the speaker is talking about himself (I/we).

In *second person*, it is the person the speaker is talking to (you).

In *third person*, the speaker is talking about another person or thing (he/she/it/they).

A verb should agree with the subject in *person*.

Some examples are

I am a student.

You are a student.

She is a student.

We wouldn't say *I are a student, you is a student, she am a student.*

Number in grammar refers to whether a word is singular or plural. For example,

I is singular.

We is plural.

It is singular.

They is plural.

Lunch is singular.

Lunches is plural.

A verb should agree with the subject in *number.*

You would say

I am a student.

We are students.

Lunch tastes good.

Lunches taste good.

You would not say *I are a student*, *we am students*, *lunch taste good*, *lunches tastes good.*

As you can see in the examples above, the spelling of a verb can change so it agrees with the subject in *person* and *number.*

The verb, *walk*, is written below to agree with the subject of each sentence in *person* and *number*. You can see the spelling changes in one place only.

Person	Singular	Plural
First Person	I *walk*.	We *walk*.
Second Person	You *walk*.	You *walk*.
Third Person	He/She/It/Jack *walks*.	They/Jack and Jim *walk*.

Now, let's look at all the changes in the verb *be* to agree with the subject of the sentence.

Person	Singular	Plural
First Person	I *am*.	We *are*.
Second Person	You *are*.	You *are*.
Third Person	He/She/It/Jack *is*.	They/Jack and Jim *are*.

COMPOUND SUBJECTS

When there are two or more nouns or pronouns the sentence is talking about, you have a compound subject.

These three things can help you so your verbs agree with compound subjects.

1. Subjects connected with *and* are plural and use a plural verb.

   Here are some examples:

   Jimmy and John *walk* to school together.

   A pencil and pen *are* needed for the exam.

   The Dragons and the Bulldogs *play* for the championship today.

2. Singular subjects connected by *or* or *nor* are singular and use a singular verb.

   Some examples are:

   Either the boss or her assistant *is* presenting the award.

   Neither Julie nor Jessica *is* going to that party.

   Chocolate or vanilla frosting *tastes* great on that cake.

3. When a compound subject has one singular subject and one plural subject connected by *or* or *nor*, the verb agrees with the closest subject.

   Here's an example:

   Either the students (plural) or the student council president (singular) *decides* (singular verb) how they will run the dance.

Note: It's usually clearer if you avoid writing a sentence with one singular and one plural subject. For example, the sentence above could be rewritten this way:

> The student council (singular) or student council president (singular) *decides* (singular verb) how they will run the dance.

WORDS COMING BETWEEN A SUBJECT AND VERB

Other words can come between the subject and verb of a sentence. The trick is to locate the actual subject and ensure the verb agrees with that.

SENTENCES WITH OTHER WORDS BETWEEN SUBJECT AND VERB	EXPLANATION
The excitement of the students *is* contagious.	*Excitement* is the subject of this sentence, not *students*. Since *excitement* is singular, the verb is singular also.
The schedule for those tests *doesn't* conflict with anything else.	*Schedule* is the singular subject, so it uses the singular verb, *doesn't*.
The many schedules of the sports teams *are set* by the Athletics Director.	The plural subject *schedules* uses a plural verb, *are set*.

INDEFINITE PRONOUNS AS SUBJECTS

Since indefinite pronouns do not refer to a specific person, place, thing or idea, some can be singular, and some are plural. When you know which indefinite pronouns are singular or plural, you can make the verb agree with them when they are the subject of a sentence.

These indefinite pronouns are singular and use a singular verb:

each	*either*	*neither*	*one*	*no one*	*nobody*
everyone	*everybody*	*anyone*	*anybody*	*someone*	*somebody*

Here are some examples:

Either of those books *satisfies* the requirements for graduation.

One of the books *is* mine.

Each of them *is* due to be returned to the library.

Everybody in Student Council positions *meets* once a week.

These indefinite pronouns are plural and use a plural verb:

both *few* *several* *many*

Here are some examples of these in sentences:

Both of my brothers *attend* a sports camp every summer.

Few of the teachers *know* about the budget change.

Many of the employees *give* to local charities.

Here's an exception, though. These indefinite pronouns can be singular or plural depending on other nouns or pronouns that may follow them:

some *any* *all* *none* *most*

When this type of pronoun is the subject of a sentence, it is often followed by other words. If there is a singular noun or pronoun in those words, the verb of the sentence should be singular.

Likewise, if there is a plural noun or pronoun in the words following the subject, the verb should be plural.

SENTENCES WITH SINGULAR INDEFINITE PRONOUNS	SENTENCES WITH PLURAL INDEFINITE PRONOUNS
Some of the cake *is going* to the children.	*Some* of my friends *are going* to the play.
Any of that evidence *seems* useful.	*Any* of those documents *seem* invaluable.
All of my artwork *has been sold.*	*All* of the tickets *have been sold.*
Most of that book *contains* information I have already studied.	*Most* of the library books *contain* valuable information.

When a verb agrees in person and number with its subject, the meaning of the sentence is clearer.

THE FOUR FORMS OF VERBS

Verb tense is the change in a verb to show when something is happening or existing. Verbs can change to show different times—present, past, or future.

To communicate different tenses, verbs usually vary in the way they are spelled and pronounced. These differences are called the **verb forms**.

There are four forms for any verb. To demonstrate, here are the four verb forms for *work*:

THE FOUR VERB FORMS	EXPLANATION
Infinitive: *(to) work*	*Work* is the basic form of the verb, called the **infinitive** form. It can also be written *to work*. In the infinitive form, *to* has no meaning; it simply has the job of indicating the infinitive form of the verb. The infinitive just communicates what the verb is saying. It doesn't show tense, number or person. Jonathan wanted *to work* all summer.

THE FOUR VERB FORMS	EXPLANATION
Present participle: *working* (often with the form of *be*)	*Working* is the present participle. A **participle** is the verb form that is used when two or more verbs act together to show different tenses. A **present participle** is formed by adding *-ing* to the infinitive. It is used with one or more verbs to form tenses that communicate continuing actions at different times. She is *working* tonight. (present) He was *working* all day yesterday. (past) Jennifer will be *working* there tomorrow. (future)
Past: *worked*	*Worked* is the past form of the verb *to work.* William *worked* for forty hours last week.
Past participle: *(have) worked*	*Worked* is the **past participle**. It is used with some form of the verb, *have,* to form tenses that communicate completed actions such as: She *has worked* in the library all morning. Sally *had worked* there for thirty years. By January, Jim *will have worked* here for one year.

When the past and past participle are formed by adding *-d* or *-ed* to the infinitive, you have a **regular verb**. Here are some examples:

FORMS OF REGULAR VERBS

Infinitive	Present Participle	Past	Past Participle
(to) work	working	worked	(have) worked
(to) talk	talking	talked	(have) talked
(to) use	using	used	(have) used
(to) date	dating	dated	(have) dated

Irregular verbs do not form the past and past participle by adding *-d* or *–ed*. They vary a lot. Let's look at some examples below.

FORMS OF COMMON IRREGULAR VERBS

Infinitive	Present Participle	Past	Past Participle
(to) be	being	was, were	(have) been
(to) begin	beginning	began	(have) begun
(to) bring	bringing	brought	(have) brought
(to) come	coming	came	(have) come
(to) do	doing	did	(have) done
(to) drink	drinking	drank	(have) drunk
(to) eat	eating	ate	(have) eaten
(to) have	having	had	(have) had

FORMS OF COMMON IRREGULAR VERBS (continued)

Infinitive	Present Participle	Past	Past Participle
(to) know	knowing	knew	(have) known
(to) run	running	ran	(have) run
(to) see	seeing	saw	(have) seen
(to) sing	singing	sang	(have) sung
(to) sit	sitting	sat	(have) sat
(to) take	taking	took	(have) taken
(to) throw	throwing	threw	(have) thrown
(to) write	writing	wrote	(have) written

Entry words in dictionaries always show the infinitive form of a verb. Following that, many dictionaries will give the past and past participle forms of an irregular verb.

When dictionaries don't give the past and participle verb forms, it is usually because they are regular verbs that are just formed by adding *-d* or *–ed* to the infinitive form.

EXERCISES 21 & 22

VERB TENSES

PRESENT TENSE

A present tense verb expresses something that is happening or existing right now.

Here are two examples:

Alex *drives* the group today.

Alex *is* a professional driver.

It is also used to talk about things in general or things that happen repeatedly.

Let's take a look:

Teachers *prepare* lessons for their students every day.

The children *wake* up at 7:00 every morning.

Below you can see the basic present tense forms of the irregular verb *sing*.

Singular	Plural
I *sing*.	We *sing*.
You *sing*.	You *sing*.
He/She/It/Jack *sings*.	They/Jack and Jim *sing*.

Below are the basic present tense forms of the irregular verb *be*.

Singular	Plural
I *am*.	We *are*.
You *are*.	You *are*.
He/She/It/Jack *is*.	They/Jack and Jim *are*.

There are three other ways to communicate that something is happening or existing in the present tense. In other words, there are three other present tenses, but you don't need to study these now. Just keep in mind that if it's happening right now from the viewpoint of the speaker or writer, it's in the present tense.

Here are some examples so you are able to recognize any present tense when you read or hear it.

SENTENCES USING OTHER PRESENT TENSES

One	
I *have studied* the assignment for discussion today. They *have fixed* breakfast for everyone.	The actions in these sentences have been completed in the present.

Two	
I *am studying* every night. They *are fixing* breakfast for everyone.	The actions in these sentences continue to be performed in the present.

SENTENCES USING OTHER PRESENT TENSES

Three	
I *have been studying* every night. They *have been fixing* breakfast for everyone all morning.	The actions in these sentences continued for a period and then were completed in the present.

EXERCISES 23 & 24

PAST TENSE

The past tense is used to communicate about something that happened or existed in the past. It uses the past form of a verb.

She *talked* to her sister yesterday.

He *wrote* a new story last month.

Jamal *took* that test last week.

We *swam* in Lake Tahoe on our vacation.

Here is what *sing* looks like in the past tense.

Person	Singular	Plural
First Person	I *sang.*	We *sang.*
Second Person	You *sang.*	You *sang.*
Third Person	He/She/It/Jack *sang.*	They/Jack and Jim *sang.*

Most questions and negative statements about the past use *did* or *didn't* + the infinitive form.

Sometimes questions use the past forms of *be* instead (*was* or *were, wasn't* or *weren't*.)

Here are examples:

Did you *go* to the game yesterday?

No, I *didn't sing* in that performance last night.

Did Sally *invite* you to her party?

Yes, but I *didn't go*.

Was she happy about it?

Weren't those cookies delicious?

As with the present tense, there are other past tenses to communicate things that happened or existed in the past. You don't need to study them now, but here are some examples so you can recognize the past tense whenever you read or hear it.

If it happened in the past from the viewpoint of the speaker or writer, it's in the past tense.

SENTENCES USING OTHER PAST TENSES

One

I *had studied* the assignment for discussion today, but *had* not *done* enough research.

They *had fixed* breakfast for everyone last week.

The actions in these sentences had been completed in the recent past.

Two

I *was studying* every night in my senior year.

She *was singing* to her son ten years ago.

They *were fixing* breakfast for everyone on the past camping trips.

The actions in these sentences continued to be performed for a time in the past.

Three

I *had been studying* every night until I graduated.

They *had been fixing* breakfast for everyone ten years ago.

The actions in these sentences continued for a period and then were completed in the past.

EXERCISES 25 & 26

THE FUTURE TENSE

The future tense is used to communicate that something will happen or exist in the future. It uses *will* + the infinitive form of a verb.

Now for some examples:

I *will apply* to that college by November 30th.

Will you *audition* for the lead role in the play?

Sam *will find* the answer to the mystery just before the book ends.

We *won't go* to the party this year. (*won't* = *will not*)

In older or more formal English, the future can be formed with *shall* + the infinitive but only in the first person.

Here are some examples with *shall*:

I *shall visit* you next month.

We *shall become* good friends.

Shall I save you a seat for the performance?

Shall we leave for the game now?

Here is what *sing* looks like in the future tense.

Person	Singular	Plural
First Person.	I *will/shall sing*.	We *will/shall sing*.
Second Person.	You *will sing*.	You *will sing*.
Third Person.	He/She/It/Jack *will sing*.	They/Jack and Jim *will sing*.

Note: Using *be* + *going* + the infinitive form of the verb is a common way to express a future action or state of being that has been decided before the time of the communication.

Examples:

I *am going to apply* to the best veterinary college.

We *are going to audition* for the lead role.

Sam *is going to find* the answer to the puzzle.

Jules and Dario *are going to contribute* to that charity.

As with the present and past tenses, there are other future tenses to communicate things happening or existing in the future. Below are some examples so you can recognize the future tense when you read or hear it.

If it's going to happen in the future from the viewpoint of the speaker or writer, it's in the future tense.

SENTENCES USING OTHER FUTURE TENSES

One	
I *will have studied* the assignment for discussion by tonight. In three hours, they *will have fixed* breakfast for everyone.	The actions in these sentences will be completed in the future.

SENTENCES USING OTHER FUTURE TENSES

Two	
I *will be studying* every night until I graduate. They *will be fixing* breakfast for everyone as long as they continue to go camping.	The actions in these sentences continue to be performed into the future.

Three	
I *will have been studying* every night for a decade by the time I become a doctor. By next year, they *will have been fixing* breakfast for everyone for ten years.	The actions in these sentences continued for a period and then will be completed in the future.

EXERCISES 27–31

PART 3

OTHER PARTS OF SPEECH

ADJECTIVES

MODIFIERS

In the earlier chapters, you learned there are parts of speech that every sentence has. A simple sentence has a noun or pronoun for the subject and a verb to tell what the subject is doing or being.

Now let's look at the parts of speech that describe other words in a sentence.

These are called modifiers. You can use them to add enthusiasm, importance, colors, size, accuracy, or any richer meaning to a sentence.

EXAMPLES OF A MODIFIER DESCRIBING ANOTHER WORD	EXPLANATION
The farm had a *red* barn.	The modifier, *red*, describes the kind of barn being talked about.
It was a *great* idea.	The modifier, *great*, describes the idea.
She swam *faster* than everyone else did.	The modifier, *faster*, describes how she swam.

A modifier can also limit the meaning of another word in a sentence.

EXAMPLES OF A MODIFIER LIMITING THE MEANING OF ANOTHER WORD	EXPLANATION
They needed to go to the store for *certain* berries.	The modifier, *certain*, limits the idea of the number or type of berries they are going to buy.
The teacher chose *two* students to give a report on the United States Supreme Court.	The modifier, *two*, limits the number of students chosen.
He *only* eats vegetables.	The modifier, *only*, limits the meaning of *eats* so we know that vegetables are all he eats.

To put that all together, a **modifier** is a word in a sentence that describes or limits the meaning of another word in the sentence.

There are two kinds of modifiers, adjectives and adverbs. Adjectives modify nouns and pronouns. Adverbs modify verbs or other modifiers.

Let's go over adjectives first.

ADJECTIVES

An **adjective** modifies a noun or pronoun. It usually answers one of these questions:

which?

how many?

what kind of?

Usually an adjective is next to the word it modifies but not always.

EXAMPLE SENTENCES WITH ADJECTIVES	EXPLANATION
That girl is running.	Which girl? The girl being pointed out. *That* is an adjective in this sentence.
Kendall has *many* friends.	How many friends? *Many* friends.
She is *younger* than Jaimie.	What kind is she? *Younger. Younger* is an adjective modifying the pronoun *she*.
I want to choose the *best* one.	Which one? The *best* one. In this sentence, *best* modifies the pronoun *one*.
Her house in Japan has paper walls.	Which house? *Her* house. In this sentence, *her* modifies the house, even though *her* may act as a pronoun in other sentences.

EXAMPLE SENTENCES WITH ADJECTIVES	EXPLANATION
That old house is *well-built* and *elegant*.	Which house? *That* house. What kind of house an *old*, *well-built*, and *elegant* house.
The *graduating* students will be honored at the *awards* ceremony.	Which students? The *graduating* students. What kind of ceremony? *Awards* ceremony.
Ten people will get up early to ski in *fresh* snow.	How many people? *Ten* people What kind of snow? *Fresh* snow.

ARTICLES

An **article** is a special type of adjective. The only articles are *a*, *an* and *the*.

Articles answer both these questions:

which?

how many?

For *a* and *an*, the answer to *how many*? is always one. If you say, "I bought *a* book" you are talking about just one book.

The answers the question *which*? because it specifies the particular person or thing named. If you say, "*The* bicycle needs to be fixed" you mean a specific bicycle that is being pointed out.

EXAMPLE SENTENCES WITH ARTICLES	EXPLANATION
I need to find *an* interesting book about *the* Civil Rights Movement in the U.S.	How many books? One book. Which Civil Rights Movement? The specific U.S. Civil Rights Movement being pointed out.
I love eating *an* apple for lunch.	How many apples? One apple.
Have you seen *the* high-tech bicycle Alex has?	Which bicycle? One specific new bicycle that Alex has.
I would like *a* racing bicycle for my birthday.	How many bicycles? Any one bicycle as long as it is for racing.

EXERCISES 1–9

ADVERBS

Let's go over the other type of modifier, the **adverb**. It modifies a verb or another modifier and usually answers one of these questions:

how?

when?

where?

to what extent?

Adverbs that modify verbs often end in *–ly* but not always.

ADVERBS THAT MODIFY A VERB	EXPLANATION
We rowed the boat *quickly*.	How did we row? *quickly*. *Quickly* modifies the verb *rowed*.
The young mother *lovingly* kissed her baby.	How did she kiss her baby? *lovingly*. *Lovingly* is an adverb that modifies the verb *kissed*.
Which of them did *better*?	Did how? *better*. *Better* is an adverb that modifies the verb *did*.

ADVERBS THAT MODIFY A VERB	EXPLANATION
I am arriving *tomorrow.*	When am I arriving? *tomorrow.* *Tomorrow* modifies the verbs of the sentence, *am arriving.*
Jason *often* helps other students with their laptops.	When does he help? *often.* *Often* modifies the verb *helps.*
They *first* found the secret entrance to the park.	When was it found? *first.* *First* modifies the verb *found.*
The family traveled *west.*	Where did the family travel? *West* *West* modifies the verb *traveled.*
The ship to Shanghai sailed *away.*	Where did the ship sail? *away.* *Away* modifies the verb *sailed.*
The athlete stepped *forward.*	Where did he step? *forward.* *Forward* modifies the verb *stepped.*
He *thoroughly* cleaned the car.	He cleaned the car to what extent? *thoroughly.* *Thoroughly* modifies the verb *cleaned.*
Our dog should *not* leave the yard.	Our dog should leave to what extent? *Not,* meaning to no extent. *Not* modifies the verbs of the sentence, *should leave.*

ADVERBS THAT MODIFY A VERB	EXPLANATION
That student has *completely* mastered tennis.	To what extent has the student mastered? *Completely.* *Completely* modifies the verb *mastered.*
We go *there frequently.*	Where do we go? *there.* When do we go? *frequently.* Both *there* and *frequently* are adverbs that modify the verb *go.*
The children walked *home happily.*	Where did they walk? *home.* How did they walk home? *happily.* Both *home* and *happily* modify the verb *walked.*
I *hardly* saw you *yesterday.*	I saw you to what extent? *hardly.* I saw you when? *yesterday.* Both *hardly* and *yesterday* modify *saw.*
Bill and Joe *never* walk *anywhere.* They *always* drive.	When do they walk? *never.* Where do they (never) walk? *anywhere.* When do they drive? *always.*
The players are improving *rapidly.* They *seldom* rest.	How are they improving? *rapidly.* When do they rest? *seldom.*

An adverb can also modify an adjective. When it does, it answers one of these questions:

to what extent?

when?

ADVERBS THAT MODIFY AN ADJECTIVE	EXPLANATION
My mother is *very* happy.	Happy to what extent? *very.* *Very* is an adverb that modifies the adjective *happy.*
The house was *completely* clean.	Clean to what extent? *completely.* *Completely* is an adverb that modifies the adjective *clean.*
There are *too* many people in the elevator.	Many to what extent? *too* (many). *Too* is an adverb that modifies the adjective *many.*
The project took *nearly* five months.	*Five* is an adjective that modifies the noun *months.* *Nearly* modifies *five* and answers the question to what extent of five months? *nearly* (five months)
My brother is *seldom* late.	*Late* is an adjective modifying brother. *Seldom* is an adverb that modifies *late* and answers the question late when? *seldom.*

ADVERBS THAT MODIFY AN ADJECTIVE	EXPLANATION
Jenny and Paul are *frequently* early.	Jenny and Paul are described by the adjective *early*. When are they early? *frequently*. *Frequently* is an adverb that modifies *early*.
The librarian makes sure that the library is *always* quiet.	The library is described by the adjective *quiet*. When is it quiet? *always*.

An adverb can modify another adverb also. Then it answers one of these questions:

to what extent?

when?

ADVERBS THAT MODIFY ANOTHER ADVERB	EXPLANATION
Race car drivers go *very* fast.	*Fast* is an adverb that modifies the verb *go*. Fast to what extent? *very (fast)*. *Very* is an adverb that modifies the adverb *fast*.

ADVERBS THAT MODIFY ANOTHER ADVERB	EXPLANATION
The cookies are *almost completely* gone.	*Completely* is an adverb that modifies the verbs *are gone*. Completely to what extent? *almost (completely).* *Almost* is an adverb that modifies the adverb *completely.*
The photographer took six photos *very quickly.*	*Quickly* is an adverb that modifies the verb took. Quickly to what extent? *very (quickly)* *Very* is an adverb that modifies the adverb *quickly.*

EXERCISES
10 & 11

PLACING MODIFIERS

To make the meaning of your sentences clearer, place modifiers next to the word they are modifying wherever possible.

Let's look at two sentences with different meanings just because the modifier is in a different place.

Only he will eat vegetables.

He will *only* eat vegetables.

Where the modifier is placed makes the difference between saying he is the only one who will eat vegetables or the only thing he will eat is vegetables.

SENTENCE ADVERBS

Sometimes an adverb modifies the whole sentence. When you run across an adverb that modifies the whole idea of a sentence, not just one word in a sentence, you have a **sentence adverb**.

Sentence adverbs are often separated from the rest of the sentence by commas.

EXAMPLE SENTENCE	EXPLANATION OF SENTENCE ADVERBS
Fortunately, the fire engine arrived on time.	*Fortunately* modifies *the fire engine arrived on time*. What is fortunate is the whole thing, not just *arrived* or *on time*.
She is, *obviously*, pretending.	*Obviously* modifies *She is pretending*. The whole thing is obvious, not just part of it.
You may take any classes that interest you. You must also study the required classes, *however*.	In this sentence, *however* is an adverb that means "in spite of that," and it modifies the whole second sentence.
Thus, I take it you agree.	*Thus* modifies *I take it you agree*.

USE ADVERBS TO MODIFY VERBS

This book covers **standard** use of English, meaning English that is generally accepted to be usual and correct.

Sometimes you'll hear or read **nonstandard** English, meaning English that is not accepted as usual and correct by most people. This is especially true in casual conversations.

For example, you may hear sentences like, "I'm doing good." *Good* is an adjective that is being used to modify a verb *doing*. Since adverbs modify verbs, in standard English the sentence would be, "I'm doing well."

When speaking or writing standard English, use an adjective to modify a noun or pronoun and an adverb to modify a verb.

NONSTANDARD USE	STANDARD USE
Elise skis *good*.	Elise skis *well*. This use is standard because the verb *skis* is modified by *well*, an adverb. *Good* is an adjective.
The choir sang very *good*.	The choir sang very *well*.
I am doing *good*.	I am doing *well*.
I want him to go *quick* and see if the mail has come.	I want him to go *quickly* and see if the mail has come. The verb *go* is modified by *quickly*, an adverb. *Quick* is an adjective.

NONSTANDARD USE	STANDARD USE
She wrote the letter *wrong* so it had to be rewritten.	She wrote the letter *wrongly* so it had to be rewritten.
	The verb *write* is modified by *wrong*, an adjective. To describe **how** she *wrote*, use the adverb *wrongly*.
He speaks *bad*.	He speaks *badly*.
	The verb *speaks* is being modified so use the adverb, *badly*.

That's how adverbs work for action verbs. It works differently when a sentence has a being verb.

The modifier following a being verb describes the *subject* of the sentence instead of the verb. Since it is modifying the subject, which is a noun or pronoun, the modifier used is an adjective.

NONSTANDARD USE	STANDARD USE
The flowers smell *beautifully*.	The flowers smell *beautiful*.
Beautifully is an adverb.	*Smell* is a being verb here so the flowers are being modified with the adjective, *beautiful*.
Compare: He performed *beautiful* at the concert.	He performed *beautifully* at the concert.
	Performed is an action verb modified by *beautifully*, an adverb.

NONSTANDARD USE	STANDARD USE
Elaine felt *well* when she won the race.	Elaine felt *good* when she won the race. *Felt* is a being verb here so Elaine is modified with an adjective, *good*.

EXERCISES
12 & 13

COMPARISON

When modifiers are used to compare two or more things, they are spelled differently.

Here are some examples using the word *tasty*.

That dinner was *tasty*. (describes the one dinner)

Yesterday's dinner was *tastier*. (compares two dinners)

New Year's dinner was the *tastiest* this year. (compares this dinner to all the others in the year)

- *Tastier* shows that two things are being compared. It is the **comparative** form of *tasty*.
- *Tastiest* shows that one thing or idea is being compared to two or more others. It is the **superlative** form of *tasty*.

Here's how it works. One-syllable modifiers use *–er* and *–est* for the comparative and superlative forms.

MODIFYING ONE THING	COMPARATIVE	SUPERLATIVE
near	*nearer*	*nearest*
The storm is *near*.	The storm is *nearer* now.	The storm is the *nearest* it has been.

MODIFYING ONE THING	COMPARATIVE	SUPERLATIVE
strong	*stronger*	*strongest*
My father is *strong.*	Your father is *stronger* than your uncle.	Jim's father is the *strongest* of all his brothers.

Two-syllable modifiers change form by using *–er* or *est,* or *more* and *most.*

MODIFYING ONE THING	COMPARATIVE	SUPERLATIVE
Easy	*easier*	*easiest*
The last problem was *easy* to solve.	Erin found it *easier* to solve than Devon did.	The first problem was the *easiest.*
ancient	*more ancient*	*most ancient*
She likes to collect *ancient* coins.	Her Roman coins are *more ancient* than her British ones.	Her Greek coin is the *most ancient* one in her collection.

If you are not sure how to spell the comparative or superlative form of a modifier, most dictionaries list them like this:

easy—adjective (*easier, easiest*).

If the *–er* or *–est* form isn't shown, it usually means that *more/most* or *less/least* are used to make the comparative or superlative forms.

Modifiers with three or more syllables use *more* and *most* or *less* and *least* for the comparative and superlative forms.

MODIFYING ONE THING	COMPARATIVE	SUPERLATIVE
happily	*more happily*	*most happily*
Sally skipped *happily* down the path.	John took on the challenge *more happily* than his brother.	Of all her memories, she thought *most happily* of the family vacation to the sea.
skillfully	*less skillfully*	*least skillfully*
The woman *skillfully* saddled her horse.	Her grandson saddled his horse *less skillfully* but successfully.	The new rider saddled her horse *least skillfully*.
ignorant	*more ignorant*	*most ignorant*
Since we always read the newspaper, we are not *ignorant* of current events.	Because he didn't like to play baseball, he was *more ignorant* about the rules of the game than his friends.	The *most ignorant* man in the world is the man who chooses not to learn.

A few common modifiers have irregular forms of comparison, so it is useful to learn them.

MODIFIER	COMPARATIVE	SUPERLATIVE
bad	worse	worst
good	better	best
well	better	best
many*	more	most
much*	more	most

EXERCISES 14 & 15

* Optional note: *Many* and *much* have similar meaning but are used differently. *Many* is used as a modifier for countable nouns, for example, *He played in* many *tournaments. Much* is used as a modifier for uncountable nouns, for example, *It doesn't take* much *flour to make cookies.*

MODIFIERS MADE FROM VERBS

Both present and past participles are forms of verbs that can act as adjectives in sentences.

As you saw in an earlier chapter, the present participles of regular verbs are formed by adding *–ing*, and the past participles have *–ed* added. The present and past participles of irregular verbs vary, but you can find them in a dictionary.

For example, the present participle of play (*playing*) or the past participle (*played*) are modifying nouns in the following sentences.

The *playing* children ran and laughed as they explored the park.

Soccer is the most *played* sport in the world.

Participles are easiest to recognize when they come before the noun or pronoun they are modifying.

PARTICIPLES THAT COME BEFORE THE NOUN OR PRONOUN THEY MODIFY	EXPLANATION
The youngest children at the party were the most *excited* ones.	The participle *excited* modifies the pronoun *ones.*
Annie will want the *painted* signs ready by tomorrow.	*Painted* modifies the noun *signs.*

PARTICIPLES THAT COME BEFORE THE NOUN OR PRONOUN THEY MODIFY	EXPLANATION
The explorers found many *sealed* jars in the ancient cave.	*Sealed* modifies the noun *jars*.
The middle school needs more *modeling* clay.	*Modeling* tells what kind of *clay*.
Eduardo always tells us *interesting* stories.	The participle *interesting* tells us what kind of *stories* he tells.
Tarzan was worried by the sound of *beating* drums.	*Beating* modifies the noun *drums*.
My guitar has a *broken* string.	*Broken* modifies the noun *string*. (*Broken* is the past participle for the irregular verb *break*.)
I spent several days revising the *written* report of my research.	*Written* is another irregular past participle that modifies *report*.

When a participle comes *after* the noun it modifies, it can be harder to recognize it as a modifier and easier to mistake it for a verb.

PARTICIPLES THAT COME AFTER THE NOUN OR PRONOUN THEY MODIFY	EXPLANATION
She could hear the ancient tree's branches *breaking* in the storm.	*Breaking* modifies the noun *branches*.
There were more letters *sent* yesterday.	*Sent* modifies the noun *letters*.

PARTICIPLES THAT COME AFTER THE NOUN OR PRONOUN THEY MODIFY	EXPLANATION
Who are the people *attending* the seminar?	*Attending* modifies the noun *people.*
The students are the ones most *appreciated.*	*Appreciated* modifies the pronoun *ones.*
Please keep a record of all books *sold.*	*Sold* modifies the noun *books.*

EXERCISES 16–19

PARTICIPIAL PHRASES

A **phrase** is a group of words acting together as one part of speech in a sentence. It does not express a complete thought.

Here are some examples of phrases:

Swimming in the ocean

Playing the game

Cooked food

Decorated room

A **participial phrase** contains a participle and acts as an adjective to modify a noun or pronoun in a sentence.

PARTICIPIAL PHRASES

Walking home, I enjoyed seeing all the spring flowers in bloom.	*Walking home* is a participial phrase that modifies the pronoun *I*.
Singing their choral program, the students realized they had prepared well for the competition.	*Singing their choral program* is a participial phrase that modifies the *students*.
Dogs *barking all night* is a common occurrence on a farm.	*Barking all night* is a participial phrase modifying *dogs*.
Food *frozen a long time* tastes stale.	*Frozen a long time* is a participial phrase modifying *food*.
Seeing himself in a mirror, the child was fascinated by his hair.	*Seeing himself in a mirror* is a participial phrase modifying *child*.
The goddess *known for her beauty* was Venus.	The participial phrase is *known for her beauty*, and it modifies *goddess*.

EXERCISES 20 & 21

PREPOSITIONS

A **preposition** is a word that shows the relationship between a noun or pronoun following it and some other word(s) in the sentence.

Here are some examples. The prepositions are in *italics*:

The boys climbed *up* the tree.

Our dog ran *across* the field.

My mother was baking cookies *for* us.

Common prepositions are:

about	*below*	*from*
above	*beneath*	*in*
across	*beside*	*into*
after	*between*	*near*
along	*beyond*	*of*
among	*by*	*off*
around	*down*	*on*
at	*during*	*out*
before	*except*	*over*
behind	*for*	*past*

since	*under*	*upon*
through	*underneath*	*with*
to	*until*	*within*
toward	*up*	*without*

Take a look at the sentences below and how a change in preposition changes the relationship between Johnny and the stream.

Johnny jumped *over* the stream.

Johnny jumped *near* the stream.

Johnny jumped *in* the stream.

PREPOSITIONAL PHRASES

Within sentences, you'll find prepositions in phrases.

You probably remember that a **phrase** is a group of words that go together and act as one part of speech in a sentence.

A **prepositional phrase** is a group of words that begins with a preposition and ends with a noun or pronoun. The whole phrase acts as an adjective if it modifies a noun, or it acts as an adverb if it modifies a verb in a sentence.

Just as an adjective or adverb does, a prepositional phrase usually answers the questions:

which?

how many?

what kind of?

how?

when?

where?

to what extent?

Let's look at the sentence, *Please go get the coats in the closet*. It has the prepositional phrase *in the closet. In the closet* modifies *coats*. It answers the question *which coats*?

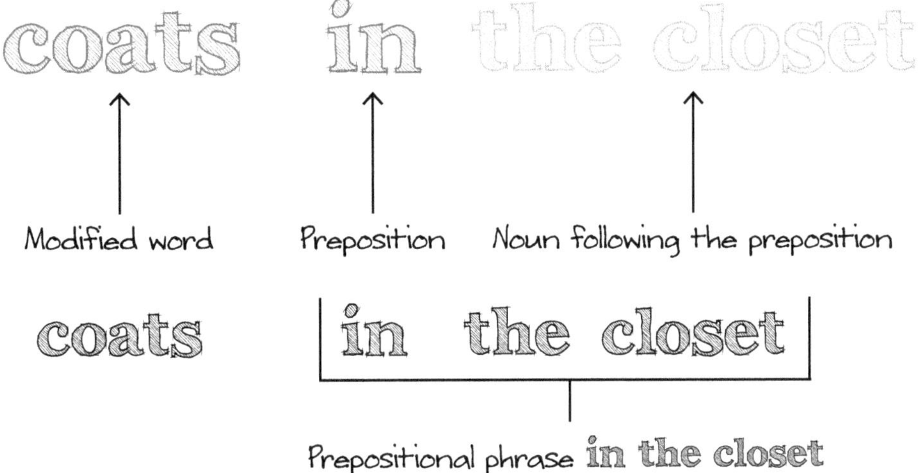

Examples of prepositional phrases:

during the long night

through France and Italy

in my opinion

to the right

along with them

PREPOSITIONAL PHRASES ACTING AS ADJECTIVES*	EXPLANATION
The professor *with an advanced chemistry degree* will be teaching my chemistry class.	Which professor? the one *with an advanced chemistry degree* *With an advanced chemistry degree* is a prepositional phrase that acts as an adjective modifying *professor.*
Everyone admired her necklace *of pearls and emeralds.*	What kind of necklace? the one *of pearls and emeralds* *Of pearls and emeralds* is a prepositional phrase that acts as an adjective modifying *necklace.*
Our group *of ten* had to wait to be seated.	How many in the group? *ten* *Of ten* is a prepositional phrase that acts as an adjective modifying *group.*
That coat *of wool* is his warmest one.	What kind of coat? the one *of wool* *Of wool* is a prepositional phrase that acts as an adjective modifying *coat.*
The woman *in the red hat* will show you where to sit.	Which woman? the one *in the red hat* *In the red hat* is a prepositional phrase that acts as an adjective modifying *woman.*

* Optional note: A prepositional phrase that acts as an adjective is called an *adjective phrase.*

PREPOSITIONAL PHRASES ACTING AS ADVERBS*	EXPLANATION
She churned the butter *by hand.*	How was the butter churned? *by hand* *By hand* is a prepositional phrase that acts as an adverb modifying *churned.*
Jonathan played the match *with great determination* and won.	How did Jonathan play? *with great determination* *With great determination* is a prepositional phrase that acts as an adverb modifying *played.*
Sylvie learned to cook *during the winter.*	When did Sylvie learn to cook? *during the winter* *During the winter* is a prepositional phrase that acts as an adverb modifying *learned.*
The ice froze *in the early morning.*	When did the ice freeze? *in the early morning* *In the early morning* is a prepositional phrase that acts as an adverb modifying *froze.*
Shay walked *on the beach* every day.	Where did Shay walk? *on the beach* *On the beach* is a prepositional phrase that acts as an adverb modifying *walked.*

* Optional note: A prepositional phrase that acts as an adverb is called an *adverb phrase.*

PREPOSITIONAL PHRASES ACTING AS ADVERBS	EXPLANATION
I put your phone *on your desk.*	Where was the phone put? *on your desk* *On your desk* is a prepositional phrase that acts as an adverb modifying *put.*
The cake was baked *to perfection.*	To what extent was the cake baked? *to perfection* *To perfection* is a prepositional phrase that acts as an adverb modifying *baked.*
The relay team ran their race *at the front of all the other runners* and won.	Where did the relay team run? *at the front* *At the front* is a prepositional phrase acting as an adverb to modify *run.* How is the *at the front* modified? *of all the other runners* *Of all the other runners* is a prepositional phrase acting as an adverb to modify the adverb phrase *at the front.*

EXERCISES
22–29

CONJUNCTIONS

A **conjunction** is a word that joins other words or groups of words.

brush *and* paint
(*and* joins two words)

across the field *but* not the river
(*but* joins two phrases)

She thought she might travel the world, *or* she would start college next year.
(*or* joins two sentences.)

Let's talk about the three main types of conjunctions.

COORDINATING CONJUNCTIONS

In grammar, **coordinate** means bring together words of equal importance.

A **coordinating conjunction** joins and relates similar words or groups of words.

I sent her flowers *and* candy.
(The word *and* connects two nouns.)

Anna was quieter *yet* wiser than most young girls were.
(The word *yet* joins two modifiers.)

Jake went home *but* Sarah stayed at the party.
(The word *but* joins two related sentences.)

And, *but* and *or* are the most common, but here's the full list of coordinating conjunctions:

for *and* *nor* *but* *or* *yet* *so*

Taking the first letter of each conjunction to spell FANBOYS is an easy way to remember these.

COORDINATING CONJUNCTIONS	
The princess was tired, *for* the night had been long.	When *for* is a conjunction, it means *because. For* is most likely used this way in poetry or older writing. When *for* means something other than *because,* it is a preposition.
The writer was finally satisfied with his book, *for* he had revised it six times.	*For* is a conjunction meaning *because* here.
You, Jose, *and* I are all going.	*And* means *also* or *in addition to. And* is always a coordinating conjunction. It is never any other part of speech.
She will not go, *nor* will she stay.	*Nor* means *and also not* or *and not either.* It is always a conjunction of one type or another.
The new student didn't win the race, *nor* did she expect to since she was the youngest runner.	*Nor* is a coordinating conjunction here.
Conrad wanted to come, *but* he couldn't.	As a coordinating conjunction, *but* is most often used to mean *in spite of this* or *on the contrary.*

COORDINATING CONJUNCTIONS

Do you want this one *or* that one?

She offered coffee *or* tea *or* milk.

Elsa wants pizza, sushi *or* steak.

When there are two or more choices, the coordinating conjunction *or* is used to introduce any choice after the first one.

It is also used in a series of items when there is a choice.

He was cold, *yet* he didn't want to go home.

As a coordinating conjunction, *yet* means *regardless of what was just said*. It introduces a second fact that may be surprising or contrary when compared to the first fact. In the example sentence, *yet* is joining two related sentences.

We were late, *so* we tried to hurry.

The fire is dying down, *so* let's throw on another log.

Jonas was hungry, *so* he fixed himself some breakfast.

We were tired, *so* we went home to rest.

There are many definitions of *so*, but when it is a coordinating conjunction, *so* means *because of this* and joins two related sentences.

All four of these example sentences use *so* as a coordinating conjunction.

EXERCISES 30–32

CORRELATIVE CONJUNCTIONS

Correlate means to connect related things.

A **correlative conjunction** is a pair of words that join equal elements of a sentence.

She is planning to go to Indonesia to teach *either* English *or* French.
(*either...or* joins two nouns)

Neither she *nor* I could solve the Headmaster's riddle in twenty-four hours.
(*neither...nor* joins two pronouns)

A professional musician needs *not only* hours of practice *but also* many skills with his instrument.
(*not only...but also* joins two phrases)

It is your decision *whether* you take a gap year *or* you go to college in September.
(*whether...or* joins two related sentences)

The correlative conjunctions are:

either...or

neither...nor

both...and

not only...but also

whether...or

CORRELATIVE CONJUNCTIONS

Either our class will set up for the party *or* they will clean up afterwards.	*Either...or* joins two sentences here.
She made that delicious meal with *neither* sugar *nor* dairy.	*Neither...nor* joins two nouns.
Nikola Tesla conceived and designed inventions in *both* radar *and* electrical technology.	*Both...and* joins two modifiers for the noun, *technology*.
He *not only* competed in the relay race *but* he *also* ran the 800-meter race and won.	*Not only...but also* joins two sentences.
She had to verify the research because she didn't know *whether* it was based on opinion *or* it was based on fact.	*Whether...or* joins two sentences.

EXERCISE 33

SUBORDINATING CONJUNCTIONS

A subordinating conjunction is the third type of conjunction. To talk about how it's used, we have to know about clauses.

A **clause** is a group of words that has a subject and its verb. There are two types of clauses, independent and dependent.

An **independent clause** expresses a complete thought and can stand alone as a sentence. Often, an independent clause is part of a bigger sentence.

Here are some examples:

Maggie runs around the track every day.
subject verb

What should we do first?
verb subject verb

The volleyball team won its game.
subject verb

A **dependent clause** has a subject and its verb but does not express a complete thought, so it leaves a person with a question. (Another name for a dependent clause is a subordinate clause.)

Let's take a look at some examples:

Because it started raining

Since we met in 2010

Whenever she could

These dependent clauses don't make sense by themselves. Look what happens when you join them with independent clauses.

Because it started raining,	the baseball team couldn't finish its game.
dependent clause	independent clause

We have been friends	since we met in 2010.
independent clause	dependent clause

She practiced her volleyball serve	whenever she could.
independent clause	dependent clause

With independent clauses, they make sense!

Now let's go back to what a subordinating conjunction is. Here **subordinate** means to treat one clause as less important than another. A **subordinating conjunction** is a word or words used to begin a dependent clause, the less important clause in a sentence. A dependent clause usually acts as an adverb in a sentence. Let's look at some examples.

After Claire finished her homework, she wrote a song for her best friend.

(*After* is the conjunction that introduces the dependent clause, *After Claire finished her homework*. It is being used as an adverb because it tells when she wrote a song.)

Joseph went to sleep early *because* he was running a marathon the next day.

(*Because* is the conjunction that introduces the dependent clause, *because he was running a marathon the next day*. It is being used as an adverb because it modifies *went to sleep*.)

Since she wanted that job, Megan studied and prepared for the job interview.

(*Since* is the conjunction that introduces the dependent clause, *Since she wanted that job.* It is being used as an adverb clause because it tells to what degree Megan studied and prepared for the job interview.)

These are some words that are commonly used as subordinating conjunctions:

after	*although*	*as*
as if	*as though*	*as long as*
because	*before*	*if*
in order that	*since*	*so that*
than	*though*	*unless*
until	*when*	*whenever*
where	*wherever*	*while*

You probably noticed that some of those words can also be used as other parts of speech. That's true! The way they are used in a particular sentence is what determines their part of speech.

SUBORDINATING CONJUNCTIONS

We sat *where* we could see all the constellations that night.

Where did we sit? *where we could see all the constellations that night.*

Where is a subordinating conjunction that begins the dependent clause *where we could see all the constellations that night.* This clause acts as an adverb modifying *sat*.

SUBORDINATING CONJUNCTIONS

The boss told Josh that he could work on inventions *when* he wanted.	When could Josh work on inventions? *when he wanted* *When* is a subordinating conjunction that begins the dependent clause *when he wanted.* This clause acts as an adverb modifying when he could work.
After she thought about her dress for the prom, she decided to wear something simple.	How did she decide? *after she thought about her dress* *After* is a subordinating conjunction here that begins the dependent clause *after she thought about her dress for the prom.* This clause acts as an adverb modifying how she decided.
John studied for his first final exam *as if* his whole future depended on it.	To what extent did John study? *as if his whole future depended on it.* *As if* is a subordinating conjunction that begins the dependent clause *as if his whole future depended on it.* This clause acts as an adverb modifying how John studied.

SUBORDINATING CONJUNCTIONS

Jane has not ridden a horse *since* she was a child.	When had Jane last ridden a horse? *since she was a child* *Since* is a subordinating conjunction that begins the dependent clause *since she was a child.* This clause acts as an adverb modifying when she had ridden.

EXERCISES 34 & 35

INTERJECTIONS

An **interjection** is a part of speech that is put between sentences or thoughts to express strong or sudden emotion. It is usually separate from a sentence and ends with an exclamation mark.

Ouch! You stepped on my foot.

Really! That's very good news.

Wow! You're a great writer!

Our team won! *Hurray for them!*

Other examples of words or phrases that can be used as interjections:

Oh!	*Hurry!*	*My goodness!*
Ah!	*Oops!*	*So sorry!*
Hey!	*Cool!*	*Good grief!*

EXERCISES
36 & 37

THE EIGHT PARTS OF SPEECH

Now you have studied all the eight parts of speech, the eight ways a word can be used in a sentence. The parts of speech are:

1. nouns
2. pronouns
3. verbs
4. adjectives (including articles)
5. adverbs
6. prepositions
7. conjunctions
8. interjections

Knowing the parts of speech can help you understand sentences more quickly and often more thoroughly.

EXERCISES 38 & 39

PART 4

THE SENTENCE

THE SENTENCE

As you know, a sentence expresses a complete thought. But how does it do that?

It starts by having a noun or pronoun that the sentence is about. This is the **subject of the sentence.** It is the noun or pronoun that is being, doing, or having something in the sentences.

They waited for their friends to arrive.

Anastasia rode horses every day when she was young.

Often there will be modifying words accompanying this noun or pronoun.

The young boy in the blue hat loved going to the beach with his parents.

The big, black dog and the little, white puppy played together often.
(This subject has two nouns *dog* and *puppy*, using the same verb.)

A sentence always has a subject, but sometimes it is not stated or written. If your mother says, "Come to the table for breakfast," you understand that she is saying it to you. *You* is the **understood subject** of that sentence.

(*You*) Please join us for my birthday.

(*You*) Enjoy!

(*You*) Let me know.

A sentence completes a thought by having a **verb of a sentence**, which is the main verb that tells what the subject is doing or being. There will usually be modifying words with this verb to tell more about the subject.*

* Optional note: Some grammar references call this the *predicate* of the sentence.

Here are some examples. The verb is in bold, and the entire part that tells about the subject of the sentence is in italics:

He ***is*** *a talented artist.*

My favorite aunt from New York ***paints*** *portraits.*

Jason ***writes*** *children's stories about animals.*

The weather ***changes*** *on a daily basis.*

SENTENCES WITH MORE THAN ONE SUBJECT OR VERB

A **compound subject** is what we call two or more subjects using the same verb in a sentence. Here **compound** means made up of two or more parts. Compound subjects are usually connected by *and* or *or.*

When there are two or more subjects, make the verb of the sentence plural.

SENTENCES WITH COMPOUND SUBJECTS

Alex and *his teammate* were running towards the ball on the field.	*Alex* and *his teammate* are two nouns the sentence is about. This sentence uses the plural verb *were running* instead of *was running.*
With their work on Student Council, *Javier, Moises,* and *Sheila* have inspired the other students.	This time the sentence has a subject with three nouns, *Javier, Moises,* and *Sheila* and uses a plural verb.
He and *I* have been friends since we were two years old.	*He* and *I* are both pronouns that this sentence is about and use a plural verb.

Similarly, a sentence can have two or more separate verbs that tell what a single subject is doing or being.

If the verbs in this kind of a sentence are in a past or future tense, there will be some groups of verbs working together. For example, *Yesterday I was visiting and was listening to music with my friends.* Sometimes this sentence will be written, *Yesterday I was visiting and listening to music with my friends.* We know part of the second verb (*was*) is there, but it isn't written. It is understood.

SENTENCES WITH TWO OR MORE VERBS FOR THE SAME SUBJECT	
Li *runs* and *kicks* the ball before the opposing player does.	This sentence has two singular verbs showing the action of one subject, Li.
Tom *will run* down field and *kick* the ball when he is in position.	This sentence has two verbs in the future tense. We know part of the second verb is there, but it isn't written. It is understood. The two verbs are really *will run* and *will kick*, but the second *will* is understood.
Susan *painted* and *framed* her portrait of her mother.	This sentence has two singular verbs showing the action of one subject, Susan.

An occasional sentence may have both a compound subject and two or more verbs. The verbs are plural when that happens.

Anna and *Tessa* both *run, swim, cycle,* and *lift* weights to train for their triathlon.

EXERCISES 1–4

CLAUSES

You could think of clauses as the building blocks of sentences.

As you learned, a **clause** is a group of words that has a subject and its verb. There are two types of clauses, independent and dependent.

An **independent clause** expresses a complete thought and can stand alone as a sentence. Often, it is part of a bigger sentence.

subject verb
My mother cooks breakfast on the weekends.

verb subject verb
What are you planning to play at your audition?

A **dependent clause** has a subject and its verb but does not express a complete thought, so it leaves a person with a question. Let's take a look at some examples.

after we ate dinner

until we graduated

since I was six years old

although it was a challenging book

These dependent clauses don't make sense by themselves, but look what happens when you join them with an independent clause.

dependent clause — independent clause
After we ate dinner, we saw a great movie.

independent clause — dependent clause
We were roommates until we graduated.

independent clause — dependent clause
I have played tennis since I was six years old.

dependent clause — independent clause
Although it was a challenging book, I loved it and learned a lot.

With independent clauses, they make sense and express a complete thought!

A dependent clause differs from a phrase. A phrase is a group of words that go together. It contains a subject or a verb but not both. Compare these phrases to similar dependent clauses.

prepositional phrase: *after the rain*
dependent clause: *after the rain stopped*
participal phrase: *swimming all morning*
dependent clause: *because they were swimming all morning*

FINDING THE SUBJECT OR VERB OF A SENTENCE

You can find the subject of a sentence by looking in the independent clause and asking, "Who or what is doing the action of the verb of the sentence?"

If the sentence has a being verb, then ask, "Who or what is existing like the being verb of the sentence?"

FINDING THE SUBJECT OF A SENTENCE

During the month of October when the leaves are falling, geese and swans noisily fly south in large flocks.	The independent clause is "geese and swans noisily fly south in large flocks." What is flying? *geese* and *swans*. That is the compound subject of the sentence.
With all the cheering, yelling, and feet pounding amid the squeak of athletic shoes in the gym, the sound of the referee's whistle seemed far away.	What is the independent clause? What seemed far away? the *sound*. That is the subject of this sentence.

FINDING THE SUBJECT OF A SENTENCE

After the shopping for ingredients and the washing, chopping, mixing and cooking, my family ate the best feast ever.	What is the independent clause? Who ate? my *family*. That is the subject of this sentence.
Despite the million and one things she had to do to prepare herself and set up other students for the ski trip, Alex was ready to leave on time at 6 a.m.	What is the independent clause? Who is ready to leave? *Alex*. That is the subject of this sentence.

Likewise, you can find the verb of a sentence by looking in the independent clause for the word telling what the subject is doing or being.

FINDING THE VERB OF A SENTENCE

During the final game of the play-offs, the soccer team and the volleyball team both played their best games.	The independent clause is *the soccer team and the volleyball team both played their best games.* What did the teams do? They *played*. That is the verb of the sentence.
Even in her first year at college, Jane was the most advanced player in the chess club.	What is the independent clause? What is the sentence saying about Jane? She *was* the most advanced player. *Was* is the verb of the sentence.

FINDING THE VERB OF A SENTENCE

Before the first performance, the cast was nervous but excited to be able to perform their play at last.	What is the sentence saying about the cast? The cast *was* nervous. *Was* is the verb of the sentence.
After practicing for months, the pianist played a difficult piece of music in the concert.	What is the sentence saying about the pianist? The pianist *played*... *Played* is the verb of the sentence.

The subject and verb can be obvious with a simple sentence. But when you are reading a long, complicated sentence, finding the subject and verb can make the difference between understanding it or not.

When learning to drive a car if it becomes necessary for young drivers to walk around the outside of the car to measure it and the distances from the sidewalk and other cars, it will be time well spent to help avoid accidents in the future.

At first glance, you may have trouble finding the subject and verb in this sentence. You could think *it becomes* is the subject and verb if you don't notice the *if* in front of it that makes it a dependent clause.

Similarly, you could think *young drivers* is the subject and *walk* and *measure* are the verbs if you don't see the preposition, *for,* in front of them.

When you know to look in the independent clause for the subject and verb of a sentence, you'll be able to find *it will be* are the subject and verb of this sentence. With a little practice, it is easy!

EXERCISES 5–12

SENTENCE ERRORS

SENTENCE FRAGMENTS

Sometimes only part of a sentence is written and the thought is not complete. This leaves a reader wondering or confused about what you're trying to say.

A **fragment** is a piece of something. A **sentence fragment** is a piece of a sentence, not a complete one. Because it isn't complete, it doesn't tell a reader your whole idea.

When you are first writing your thoughts down, you might write a sentence fragment because you know what you are trying to say. But you'll want to find and fix any sentence fragments before giving your writing to someone to read so they will know your complete thought.

To fix a sentence fragment, complete the thought by making sure there is a subject and a verb of the sentence. Let's look at some examples.

SENTENCE FRAGMENTS	COMPLETE SENTENCES
Before the rain (This is incomplete because it is a prepositional phrase.)	I went for a long walk before the rain. An independent clause was added to complete the thought by saying what happened *before the rain*.

SENTENCE FRAGMENTS	COMPLETE SENTENCES
Since Sebastien beat everyone running down the field (This is incomplete because it is a dependent clause.)	Since Sebastien beat everyone running down the field, *he was able to score a goal.* An independent clause was added to complete the sentence.
The basketball player who was running down the court as fast as he could (This is an incomplete independent clause.)	The basketball player who was running down the court as fast as he could *made a basket and scored two points.* The thought was fully completed.
Even though the tennis player served the ball well (This is incomplete because it is a dependent clause.)	Even though the tennis player served the ball well, *she was unable to win the match.* An independent clause was added.
Because the dog spotted some wild turkeys (This is incomplete because it is a dependent clause.)	Because the dog spotted some wild turkeys, *she ran across the field.* An independent clause was added.
Around the campus (This is a prepositional phrase.)	*The students picked up trash* around the campus. An independent clause was added to make a complete thought.

RUN-ON SENTENCES

Sometimes you may put two or more complete sentences together without a needed conjunction or period. That makes a **run-on sentence.**

It may be understandable to you because you know what you are trying to say. However, very often readers find run-on sentences confusing because they aren't sure what you are trying to say, and your ideas can get lost. So, you can help your readers by finding and fixing any run-on sentences before giving them your writing.

Usually adding periods or conjunctions will take care of run-on sentences.

RUN-ON SENTENCES	REVISED SENTENCES
Sebastien beat everyone running down the field, he kicked the ball into the goal.	Sebastien beat everyone running down the field, *so* he kicked the ball into the goal. (A conjunction was added.)
Even though the tennis player served the ball well, it went out of bounds at the last second, she threw down her racket in frustration, she knew the umpire would give her a penalty for it.	Even though the tennis player served the ball well, it went out of bounds at the last second. She threw down her racket in frustration, *even though* she knew the umpire would give her a penalty for it. (A period and a conjunction were added.)

RUN-ON SENTENCES	REVISED SENTENCES
The dog spotted some wild turkeys, so she ran across the field to chase them for fun, after forcing them to fly into nearby trees, she barked at them, so they were afraid to come down for hours.	The dog spotted some wild turkeys, so she ran across the field to chase them for fun. She forced them to fly into nearby trees, *but* she barked at them, so they were afraid to come down for hours. (A period and a conjunction were added.)
He ate pizza, she had a milkshake, the kids ate chicken nuggets.	He ate pizza. She had a milkshake. The kids ate chicken nuggets. (Periods were added.) Or He ate pizza, *and* she had a milkshake. The kids ate chicken nuggets. (A conjunction and a period were added.)

When you write sentences without these errors, your readers will understand your ideas without any difficulty.

EXERCISES 13–16

THREE WAYS TO BUILD A SENTENCE

You can build sentences different ways to vary their lengths and types. When you do this, your writing can be made more interesting and more enjoyable to read. Instead of this:

> *The soccer team plays an important game today. They have a tough opponent. It will be a night game. The team is practicing longer today. They are confident. They can win this game. I cannot wait to see it.*

You could have this:

> *The soccer team plays an important game today, and they have a tough opponent. It will be night game, so the team is practicing longer today. They are confident that they can win this game. I cannot wait to see it.*

The second paragraph has these three types of sentences:

1. A **simple sentence** has a subject and its verb and expresses a complete thought.

   Most people ate cake at the birthday party.

   Sebastien kicked the ball into the goal.

   The tennis player served the ball well.

   The dog ran across the field for fun.

2. By combining different clauses, you can say more. A sentence made up of two or more independent clauses connected by a conjunction is a **compound sentence**.

   Most people ate cake at the birthday party, and some guests played games, but we all gave our friend gifts.

   Sebastien beat everyone running down the field, and he kicked the ball into the goal.

   The tennis player served the ball well, but it went out of bounds at the last second.

   The dog spotted some wild turkeys, and she ran across the field to chase them for fun.

3. When you combine an independent clause with a dependent clause, it makes a **complex sentence**.

   Since Sebastien beat everyone running down the field, he was able to kick the ball into the goal.

   Even though the tennis player served the ball well, it went out of bounds at the last second.

   The dog ran across the field for fun because she spotted some wild turkeys to chase.

Have some fun making your writing more interesting by mixing in all these types of sentences.

EXERCISES 17–21

PART 5

JOBS NOUNS AND PRONOUNS DO IN SENTENCES

JOBS NOUNS AND PRONOUNS DO IN SENTENCES

Nouns and pronouns can be used in different ways in sentences. *Jobs* is a way to describe these different uses. An example of a job would be a noun that is used as the subject of a sentence.

We'll cover five different ways nouns and pronouns can be used in sentences, starting with the subject of a sentence.

THE SUBJECT OF A SENTENCE

Earlier chapters covered the simple subject of a sentence and how to find it.

As you know, the main noun or pronoun that the sentence is talking about is the **simple subject.** It is the noun or pronoun that is being, doing, or having something in the sentence.

EXAMPLE SENTENCES	SIMPLE SUBJECTS
Rio plays the piano well.	Who plays well? *Rio*
The *skill* of simple coding can be learned in a few weeks.	What can be learned? *skill*
What did the *students play* ?	Who played something? *students*
You own a nice motorcycle.	Who owns a motorcycle? *You*

EXAMPLE SENTENCES	SIMPLE SUBJECTS
There are beautiful, spring *flowers* all along the path.	What are there? *Flowers*
Sing this song to me, please.	Who sings the song? *You* (understood subject)
Ying and *Margaux* practiced all night.	Who practiced? *Ying* and *Margaux* (compound subject)

Often there will be other words with the simple subject. All that together makes the **complete subject.**

EXAMPLE SENTENCES	COMPLETE SUBJECTS
The youngest son of my best friend's family plays football well.	*Son* is the simple subject. *The youngest son of my best friend's family* is the complete subject.
Many people carrying backpacks and lunches hiked up the trail to the pond.	*People* is the simple subject. *Many people carrying backpacks and lunches* is the complete subject.
Tonight, the student-run play of the year will be a comedy about two writers.	*Play* is the simple subject, and *the student-run play of the year* is the complete subject. *Tonight* isn't part of the complete subject because it is an adverb modifying the whole sentence not just the subject.

What are all these other words with the simple subject? They can be modifiers, conjunctions, phrases, dependent clauses and more. Take a look at these examples with the complete subject in italics.

Tonight, *the student-run play of the year* will be a comedy about two writers.

art. adj. simp. subject prep. phr.

The teenager driving a car for the first time did very well.

art. simp. subject participial phr. prep. phr.

Those who wanted to get ahead attended all the study halls.

simp. subj. dependent clause

When you can spot the entire complete subject of a sentence, it is easier to correctly spot or write the main verb of a sentence.

Take a look at this sentence. You might think that *carrying* is the verb, but it actually isn't. If you spot the complete subject, you'll see the verb of the sentence is *hiked*.

Many people carrying backpacks and lunches hiked up the trail to the pond.

adj. simple subj. participial phrase

EXERCISES 1–4

DIRECT OBJECTS

Direct objects are another way nouns and pronouns are used in sentences.

An **object** is the noun or pronoun that is affected by the action of the verb or is affected by the relationship expressed by a preposition. A **direct object** tells what the action of the verb is directed to, acted on, or resulted in. A sentence can have more than one direct object, or it can have none.

You can find the direct object in a sentence by asking *who?* or *what? is being affected by* the action of a verb. The direct object is usually after the verb of the sentence.

You will only see direct objects with action verbs.

SENTENCE	DIRECT OBJECT
Neo dropped the *ball.*	The direct object is *ball* because it answers the question *Neo dropped what?*
My aunt answered my *mother.*	The direct object is *mother* because it answers the question *My aunt answered whom?*
Sophie is making *dumplings.*	The direct object is *dumplings* because it answers the question *Sophie is making what?*

SENTENCE	DIRECT OBJECT
That writer owns both a *typewriter* and a *computer.*	The two direct objects *typewriter* and *computer* are things the subject (writer) is having, and they answer the question *That writer owns what?*
Omar hit *it* in the center.	*It* is the direct object, and answers the question *Omar hit what?*
Imani hit *herself* on the knee.	The direct object is *herself* because it answers the question *Imani hit whom?*

If something is simply being, there is no action taking place so being verbs don't have direct objects. Let's see how this works in sentences with being verbs.

He was the best player on the team.

I became a doctor after ten years of study and internship.

They seem complacent all the time.

Even though a noun follows the being verb, it is just describing what the subject of the sentence is being.

You will never see a direct object in a prepositional phrase. You can compare these sentences to see the difference.

SENTENCES WITH DIRECT OBJECTS	SENTENCES WITH PREPOSITIONAL PHRASES
The children played the *piano.*	The children played *on the piano.*
In this sentence, *played* is a transitive verb. It has a direct object (*piano*) that receives the action.	In this sentence, *on the piano* is a prepositional phrase, so *piano* is not a direct object.
We can meet *her* for lunch.	We can meet *with her* for lunch.
Her is a direct object. It receives the action of the verb *meet,* which is a transitive verb in this sentence.	In this sentence, *with her* is a prepositional phrase, so *her* is not a direct object.
He pushed the *door* open.	He pushed *on the door.*
Door is the direct object because that is what he *pushed.* That means *pushed* is transitive.	In this sentence, *on the door* is a prepositional phrase, so *door* is not a direct object.

So, only look for direct objects with action verbs.

EXERCISES
5–8

INDIRECT OBJECTS

The **indirect object** is the noun or pronoun in a sentence that tells who or what the action of the verb is being done for. It answers the question *who* or *what* the action is done for.

The indirect object of the verb always comes before the direct object. A sentence only has an indirect object if there is also a direct object.

John gave me candy.

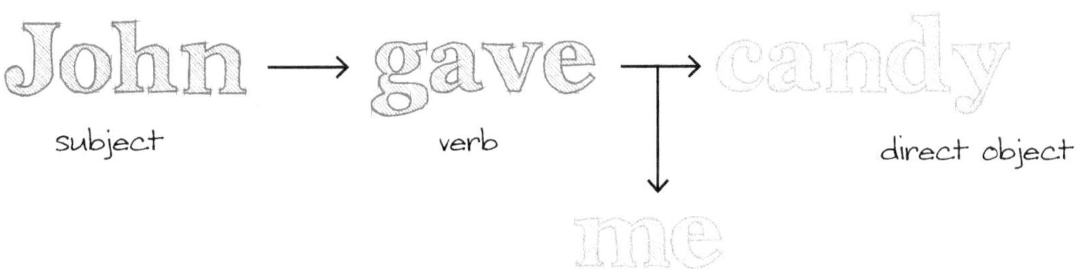

SENTENCE	DIRECT OBJECT	INDIRECT OBJECT
I mailed *her* the money.	*Money* is what was mailed.	Who was the money mailed to? *her*
Cameron gave the *garden* a good watering.	*Watering* is what is being given.	What got the watering? *Garden*

SENTENCE	DIRECT OBJECT	INDIRECT OBJECT
They handed *him* and *Kahlil* books from the library.	*Books* is what was handed.	Who was handed the books? *him* and *Kahlil* (two indirect objects)
The rider gave the *horse* a carrot on his back.	*Carrot* is what was given.	What got a carrot? *horse*
Sasha and Dimitri taught *themselves* rock climbing when they were quite young.	*Rock climbing* is what was taught.	Who was taught? *themselves*

Once you find the direct object, the indirect object will be easier to spot.

EXERCISES
9–12

THE OBJECT OF A PREPOSITION

Here is another job a noun or pronoun can do in sentences.

As you know, a **preposition** is a word that shows the relationship between the noun or pronoun following it and some other word(s) in the sentence. The **object of a preposition** is the noun or pronoun that is affected by the preposition it follows.

Kasem ran *down* the *hill.*
prep. object of preposition

Paola read her book *in* the *library.*
prep. object of preposition

She threw the ball *to* *Raynor.*
prep. object of preposition

The train went *through the beautiful countryside* *of* *Vietnam and Thailand.*
prep. obj. of prep. prep. objects of prep.

After *the movie,* they went to eat dinner.
prep. obj. of prep.

As you can see, the object of a preposition is the noun or pronoun that ends a prepositional phrase.

The object of a preposition is different from a direct or indirect object of a sentence. Those are never in a prepositional phrase. Here are some examples showing how the different objects are used.

My friend gave	me	a protein bar	during	the *game.*
	indirect obj.	direct obj.	prep.	obj. of prep.

Our teacher gave	us	a fun assignment to do	over	the *break.*
	indirect obj.	direct object	prep.	obj. of prep.

Whenever you see a prepositional phrase, there will be an object of the preposition at the end of it.

EXERCISES 13–16

THE NOUN RESTATEMENT

Here's the last job a noun or pronoun can do in a sentence.

A **noun restatement** is a noun or pronoun that states something again in a different way. It can restate, rename, or identify a previously stated noun or pronoun.*

SENTENCE	NOUN RESTATEMENT
Last night I finished reading my literature seminar book, *my favorite book of all time.*	*My favorite book of all time* is the noun restatement that restates what *my literature seminar book* is.
Please keep an eye on my dog, *Totoro.*	*Totoro* is the noun restatement. It renames the previous noun, *dog.*
After lunch, we will meet my brother, *Alejandro.*	*Alejandro* is a noun restatement that identifies which *brother.*
Nadine gave the book to Matteo, the *one* who should have gotten it before.	*One* is the noun restatement. It is a pronoun that renames *Matteo.*

* Optional note: Some grammar references call the noun restatement that immediately follows the noun being renamed an *appositive*.

SENTENCE	NOUN RESTATEMENT
"Hi, it's me, your favorite *cousin*!"	Occasionally you will find pronoun restatements as well as noun restatements, but we will call them both by the same name. *Cousin* is a noun restatement that identifies the pronoun *me*.

SUBJECT RESTATEMENT*

The noun restatements you have seen so far all come right after the noun or pronoun they rename. There is another type of noun restatement called a subject restatement.

A **subject restatement** is a noun or pronoun in the sentence that restates, renames or more fully identifies the subject of a sentence.

A subject restatement always follows being verbs such as:

is	*am*	*are*	*was*	*were*	*will be*
become	*becomes*	*became*	*is being*	*is becoming*	*might be*

* Optional note: Some grammar references call a subject restatement that follows the verb a *predicate nominative*.

So you'll see a being verb in each of the examples below.

SENTENCE	SUBJECT RESTATEMENT
After all, Skipper is the fastest *dog* in town.	*Dog* is a subject restatement that re-identifies the subject, *Skipper.*
Ilona is an exceptional *athlete.*	*Athlete* is a subject restatement that renames the subject, *Ilona.*
Our best players are *Hailey* and *Tiana.*	Both *Hailey* and Tiana are subject restatements that identify the subject *players.*
Her brother is the famous *ballet dancer.*	*Ballet dancer* is a subject restatement that renames the subject, *brother.*
All of the children are *Cub Scouts.*	*Cub Scouts* is a subject restatement for the subject *All* (not *children*, which is the object of the preposition).
Amelie became a *doctor.*	*Doctor* is a subject restatement for *Amelie.*

EXERCISES 17-22

VERBS CAN ACT AS NOUNS

Certain forms of verbs can act as nouns in sentences.

A present participle (such as *playing*) or the infinitive (such as *to play*) may be used as a noun in a sentence.*

These verb forms can do any of the jobs of a noun or pronoun in a sentence. They can be a subject, a direct object, an indirect object, an object of a preposition, or a noun restatement.

VERB FORMS	EXPLANATION
Playing on our team requires both skill and the intention to win.	The noun *playing* is the subject of the sentence.
The children like *to play*.	*To play* is the direct object. The children like *what? to play*
Nisha gives *sailing* her full attention.	The verbal noun *sailing* is the indirect object and *attention* is the direct object. Nisha gives her full attention *to what? sailing*
Some people have a problem with *seeing* close up.	*Seeing* is the object of the preposition *with*.

* Optional note: Other grammar references call a verb form acting as a noun a *gerund* or a *verbal noun*.

VERB FORMS	EXPLANATION
To see is *to believe.*	There are two verb forms in this example. The subject is *To see* and the noun restatement is *to believe,* which restates *To see.*
It's a good idea *to organize* during the *planning.*	*To organize* is a noun restatement that restates *idea. Planning* is the object of the preposition *during.*

As you can see, these verb forms are doing the same jobs as a noun, even though they are formed from a verb.

You can see the infinitive of a verb working as a noun above. When the infinitive of a verb is used with *to,* it is an **infinitive phrase**. Just be sure to differentiate an infinitive phrase from a prepositional phrase when it has the word *to.*

An infinitive phrase will always have *to* + a verb, for example, *to work.*

You can tell when *to* is a preposition because it will be *to* + a noun, for example, *to school.*

Infinitive Phrases	Prepositional Phrases
to go	to the ocean
to fly	to him
to become	to Sao Paulo

This will explain those sentences where you see a verb form doing the job a noun would normally do.

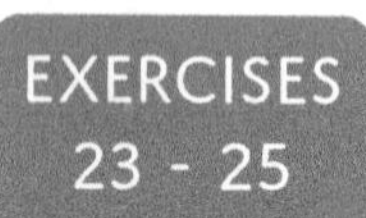

PART 6

WHAT IS CASE?

WHAT IS CASE?

Case is a grammar term that refers to the different forms a noun or pronoun can take depending on what job it's doing in a sentence. This chapter will cover three different forms that nouns and pronouns take when they are used in a specific way in the sentence.

The examples below show each one of these three cases. They are all talking about Rahim, but pronouns have been used to replace his name, so you can see how they change with each case.

He is a good basketball player.
(*He* is the pronoun used as a subject.)

The team captain threw the ball to *him*.
(*Him* is the pronoun used as an object.)

Whose handwriting is the best? *His* is the best.
(*His* is the pronoun used to show possession.)

Nouns don't change much in English, but most pronouns have different forms for each case.

THE POSSESSIVE CASE

When a noun or pronoun shows ownership, it is in the **possessive case**.

The possessive case is the only case where nouns change form, by adding an apostrophe and s ('s). When used as a subject or object, nouns don't change. Look at these examples.

(possessive case) The colors of the carpet match the *table's*.

(subject) The *table* is stored in the garage.

(object) He put his books on the *table*.

Let's look at different examples of nouns in the possessive case:

Last night, we stayed at *Lacey's*.

Does anyone know whose hat this is? It is that *man's*.

Whose laptops are these? They are the *students'*.
(When the plural noun ends in s, only add an apostrophe.)

A pronoun in the possessive case has different forms. Take a look at these examples.

	SINGULAR	PLURAL
first person	That is *mine.*	*Ours* is the red one.
second person	Which one is *yours*?	Which one is *yours*?
third person	*Hers* is the green one. *Whose* *His* *Its*	*Theirs* are the books I need. *Whose*

The possessive pronouns are *mine, yours, his, hers, its, theirs, whose,* and *ours.*

Don't confuse these with modifiers that show possession such as *my, your, his, her, our,* and *their.* These are not pronouns that replace a noun. Take a look at the difference.

Pronoun in possessive case:	That one is *mine.*
Modifier showing possession:	*My* house is on the next street.
Pronoun in possessive case:	*His* is the blue one.
Modifier showing possession:	I like *his* hat.

EXERCISES 2–5

THE NOMINATIVE CASE

When a pronoun acts as a subject of a sentence or clause, it is in the nominative case*. Nominative comes from the Latin word for *naming*. It applies to the subject of a sentence, which names what the sentence is about. These are the forms of pronouns used as subjects: *I, you, he, she, it, we, they,* and *who.*

Knowing this you will know which pronoun to use in your sentences.

INCORRECT	CORRECT
Ashanti and *me* are going to the library now.	Ashanti and *I* are going to the library now.
Them are playing a challenging match today.	*They* are playing a challenging match today.
Whom is that teacher over there?	*Who* is that teacher over there?

For most pronouns, this is straightforward. Knowing when to use *who* versus *whom* can be trickier so there will be more about that in the next chapter.

* Optional note: Some grammar references may call this the *subjective case.*

SUBJECT RESTATEMENTS

When there is a sentence with *it* as a subject, the pronoun that is a subject restatement should be in the nominative case, the same case as the subject.

That is why the grammatical answer to the question *Who wrote this essay?* is *It was I.* Most people would actually say, *It was me,* so there is agreement that it's acceptable to say it that way.

If you want to speak or write formally, however, use the pronoun that is restating a subject in the nominative case. Let's look at more examples.

Who was responsible? It was *she.*

Who is there? It is *I.*

THE OBJECTIVE CASE

When a word acts as an object, it is in the objective case. As mentioned earlier, nouns don't change in the objective case, but pronouns do.

A pronoun will be in the objective case when it acts as a direct object, an indirect object or an object of a preposition in a sentence. The forms of pronouns used as objects are: *me, you, him, her, it, us, them,* and *whom*.

Let's take a look at examples:

TYPE OF OBJECT	INCORRECT	CORRECT
Direct object	You can find *she* in the office.	You can find *her* in the office.
Indirect object	My father gave my brother and *I* diving lessons.	My father gave my brother and *me* diving lessons.
Object of a preposition	He wanted to talk to Devansh and *I*.	He wanted to talk to Devansh and *me*.

WHO/WHOM

Where should you use who and where should it be whom? This question comes up in writing, even though it also applies to spoken English. Often when people are speaking, they use who, whether it is correct or not.

If you want to use who and whom correctly, you just have to know two things. First, *who* is a nominative pronoun, so it is used as a subject. It can be the subject of a sentence or a clause.

Who is coming to dinner?

The artist, who created the movie *Human Flow,* is Ai Weiwei.

Second, *whom* is an objective pronoun, so it is used as an object of a verb or preposition. When whom follows the verb or preposition it is the object for, it is easier to see that you should use it. However, whom often comes before the verb or preposition.

Whom did you choose to sing a solo?

Whom should I send invitations to?

Her mother, *whom* I have never seen, sent me a beautiful card.

Is whom used correctly in those sentences? If you're not sure whether to use whom or not, you can change the order of words in the question or clause to see if whom is an object.

EXAMPLE	EXPLANATION
Whom did you choose to sing a solo?	You choose *whom* to sing a solo. *Whom* is the object of *choose.*

EXAMPLE	EXPLANATION
Whom should I send invitations to?	I should send invitations to *whom*. *Whom* is the object of the preposition *to*.
Her mother, whom I have never seen, sent me a beautiful card.	*Her mother, I have never seen whom, sent me a beautiful card.* *Whom is the object of the verb seen.*

With some practice, you'll always know when to use objective pronouns.

ALL CASES

As you have seen, nouns only change by adding 's in the possessive case.

Most pronouns have different forms for each case. Here are all the forms of pronouns for all three cases.

nominative case	objective case	possessive case
I	*me*	*mine*
you	*you*	*yours*
he	*him*	*his*
she	*her*	*hers*
it	*it*	*its*
we	*us*	*ours*
they	*them*	*theirs*
who	*whom*	*whose*

Now that you know about the cases, you'll know when to use each pronoun.

INDEX

E

G

I

M

N

CPSIA information can be obtained
at www.ICGtesting.com
Printed in the USA
BVHW060746141122
651490BV00001B/3

9 780897 391177